Henley, Thatcher, and Nolan Learn About Jesus' Love

By Pam Bass

Children were brought by
Mommies and daddies

To see Jesus
With ease.

To Jesus, they
wanted to greet.

as well as to meet.

Children were brought
To Jesus by
Mommies and daddies
To see Jesus
With ease.

To Jesus they
Wanted to meet,
As well as
To greet.

Jesus' helpers saw them,

Saying to get away from Him.

Children were brought
To Jesus by
Mommies and daddies
To see Jesus
With ease.

To Jesus they
Wanted to meet,
As well as
To greet.

Jesus' helpers
Saw them
Saying get away
From Him.

The helpers were shooing,

Jesus was pursuing.

Children were brought
To Jesus by
Mommies and daddies
To see Jesus
With ease.

To Jesus they
Wanted to meet,
As well as
To greet.

Jesus' helpers
Saw them
Saying get away
From Him.

The helpers
Were shooing,
Jesus was
Pursuing.

Jesus said, "Let the children Come to me."

Let them be.

Children were brought
To Jesus by
Mommies and daddies
To see Jesus
With ease.

To Jesus they
Wanted to meet,
As well as
To greet.

Jesus' helpers
Saw them
Saying get away
From Him.

The helpers
Were shooing,
Jesus was
Pursuing.

Jesus said, "Let the
Children come to me."
Let them be.

Jesus hugged them

And talked with them.

Children were brought
To Jesus by
Mommies and daddies
To see Jesus
With ease.

To Jesus they
Wanted to meet,
As well as
To greet.

Jesus' helpers
Saw them
Saying get away
From Him.

The helpers
Were shooing,
Jesus was
Pursuing.

Jesus said, "Let the
Children come to me."
Let them be.

Jesus hugged them
And talked with them.

Children are loved by Him.

He spends time with them.

Children were brought
To Jesus by
Mommies and daddies
To see Jesus
With ease.

To Jesus they
Wanted to meet,
As well as
To greet.

Jesus' helpers
Saw them
Saying get away
From Him.

The helpers
Were shooing,
Jesus was
Pursuing.

Jesus said, "Let the
Children come to me."
Let them be.

Jesus hugged them
And talked with them.

Children are loved by Him.
He spends time with them.

Henley, Thatcher, and Nolan
learn Jesus loves them a lot.
Their mommy and daddy tell
them so.
The Bible (God's special book)
tells them so.
Henley, Thatcher, and Nolan
love Jesus a whole lot.

"Let the children
come to me."
Mark 10:14b (NIV)

How do you know
Jesus loves you?